# 15 MINUTE AGENCY

How to sign your first 4-figure marketing client in as little as 15 minutes, even as a total beginner with zero sales experience

JORDAN PLATTEN

# Contents

# Frequently Asked Questions

### Do I need money to get started?

No. Being a service-based business, Social Media Marketing requires no financial investment in order to get started. All you simply need is a willingness to learn and the hunger to change your life.

### Will this work in my country?

Yes! Regardless of where you are in the world, all businesses require marketing in order to promote their services and stay ahead of the competition. Whilst earnings may vary from country to country, if Social Media is an active part of your culture, you can make this work.

### Do I need to have previous experience?

No. Whilst it's important to understand the ins and outs of the business model, which you'll learn inside this book, you don't need any experience prior to getting started.

### Can I do this whilst travelling?

You certainly can. As long as you have access to the internet, you can manage your business from anywhere, be it lounging on a beach in Bora Bora or even backpacking through Cambodia. In the first year of launching my agency, I had 7 vacations and not once struggled to keep on top of business.

### Can I do this alongside a 9-5 or full time education?

Absolutely. When I first started, I was leaving for work at 8am and not getting home until 6pm. In this book you will learn how I managed to secure my first £2,000 of profit within two weeks whilst working full time. Whether you want to sack your boss and achieve financial freedom or even just earn some extra cash whilst studying, this book is for you.

# Who Am I

I'm Jordan Platten, an entrepreneur from the UK, who by the age of 23 had established a six figure marketing agency with a string of international clients. As my business continued to grow, I made it my mission to help others achieve financial freedom, escape the 9 to 5 and live life on their own terms. My road to success has been long, challenging and has involved a lot of hard work. Before I show you how I grew my agency and how you can too, here's how I started...

I was kicked out of university so I thought I'd better work my way up the corporate ladder. It wasn't long until I was trying to figure out how to escape employment. My whole life I'd wanted to launch my own business, so I wouldn't have to answer to anyone. I wanted to be able to live life on my own terms and spend my time with friends and family, doing the things I love the most.

The thing was, for the life of me, I couldn't think of a business idea and without that, I'd never be able to quit my job, let alone achieve financial freedom.

To make things worse, I felt terrible because I was living in this constant cycle of working, eating and sleeping. I felt even worse because success was all around me, everywhere I looked, I just couldn't reach it. I felt like a failure. I was living for the weekends, spending my life saving for one holiday a year that was over before it had even started. If I didn't find a way out, I was on the verge of depression.

Then, as if by chance, something amazing happened...

I was working away again; back at the hotel after a long day, tired, trying to rack my brains on how I could escape the cycle I was in. That's when I got a call from a friend who told me that he'd made twenty thousand pounds that month.

Six months prior to that call, I was sat next to that same friend in a call centre. One morning, he walked into the office with a smile on his face, paper in hand and told me he was handing in his resignation. He told me he was going to start an online business, by recommendation of someone he'd met who was 'making thousands' from managing social media pages for companies. At the time, I doubted him, thinking to myself *that's never going to work*. Boy did he prove me wrong.

After that call, it was crystal clear to me where I was going wrong all this time. I was so strung up on trying to find the next 'big thing', the next Uber, that I failed to look at what was right under my nose.

I learned that you don't need to reinvent the wheel to be successful; you just need to learn to solve problems.

As a result of his call, I immersed myself tirelessly in 'social media marketing', I committed all my time to learning the ins and outs of the industry.

After doing this, I managed to quit my job within two weeks—less than a month after our phone call. Suddenly, I was earning more than double my old salary for less than half the hours, and I was hungry for more.

My plan was to start reaching out to all the businesses in my local area. So, I started making a list of all companies within a 20 mile radius of my house. I then started calling those companies and arranging meetings with their owners so I could pitch my service.

However there was a problem… Even though I managed to get my feet off the ground pretty quickly, I found myself spending all week calling up businesses to speak to maybe one or two owners. Even when I did manage to secure meetings, I felt like it took me hours to close the deal. I ended up getting so frustrated that I decided to take two full weeks off to create a better system, re-writing everything I thought I knew, to help sign new clients not in weeks, days or hours… but in just minutes.

I chose to call it 'The 15 Minute Strategy'. I thought If I could create something that would make it possible to help people in the same position I was in—stuck in a full time job or just in the pursuit for a better life—then I'd be really happy.

After signing multiple 6 figures of business in less than a year, using this new system, I wrote The 15 Minute Agency.

Once I had cemented how the system worked, I started to let other aspiring entrepreneurs use my system. Consequently I've been able to help hundreds of people sign clients, and ultimately quit their jobs, achieve financial freedom and most importantly - live life on their own terms.

## Why Social Media Marketing Is The Most In Demand Service On The Planet

Social Media is one of the most effective tools that you can use to reach your target audience. When implemented effectively, a social strategy can achieve many different goals; such as increasing subscriptions, boosting sales and driving traffic to specific web pages. Yet all of this wouldn't be possible without the internet. Even though some love it and others hate it, the internet has to be one of the most valuable tools for business owners. Since it was introduced back in 1983, it has transformed the way we communicate. Basic things such as buying a gift, starting a business or even sharing a photo or video with a friend were all made possible with just a few clicks.

Before the internet was introduced, if you wanted to keep up to date with news you had to read the local paper or tune in to the radio. If you wanted to buy something you would have to go to the high street and search for what you need, or if you needed to research something, trawling through the library was your best option. Online businesses didn't exist, and social media was unheard of.

In the very early days of the internet, it was designed to send small amounts of data between two terminals and was a highly complex system which was managed by a team of elite coding professionals. Compare that with today where the internet is a vast, global resource with an endless stream of content being accessed, shared and uploaded every second. Everyone has the ability to create, share and comment on any type of online content. Social media has taken this a step further and is now one of the best ways that businesses can build trust and develop a loyal following.

While the internet was welcomed by many, it did have its sceptics. In the early days of the internet, it didn't really have a structure and search engines such as Google didn't exist. So, it was understandable that some believed the internet was simply a fad or it would phase out to nothing. But the critics were proved wrong. The internet only grew stronger and evolved as the years passed by. In the early 21st Century Web 2.0 was released, and this brought a whole new dimension to the internet, introducing social media and interactive tools which many of us use to communicate today. The internet was no longer simply an avenue to exchange information; it was an advanced tool that allowed individuals from all over the world to buy products, watch videos, search for information and communicate. Today, we can communicate with clients on the other side of the world in a matter of seconds. Personal stories can be shared globally, and local businesses can grow to reach international audiences.

The internet has allowed all types of business to thrive and not just those that exist online. Your local restaurant, dentist and even the yoga studio down the street are all benefiting from the internet right now. How? Social media marketing.

Through growing a following on popular social platforms, establishing credibility and building trust, business owners are able to target a much wider audience. As businesses continue to build their community, they can share promotions, distribute quality content and provide first class customer service.

As the capabilities of the internet are realised, you can leverage the tools and technologies to help your business grow, whatever industry you are in. Businesses who started out creating websites are now making thousands from their efforts. If you are not using the internet as part of your marketing strategy today, you are leaving thousands of pounds on the table. Even though the sceptics from the early days of the internet eventually followed suit, they already missed out on years of potential earnings and opportunities.

So how exactly can you build a profitable and flexible income from all of this? I'll get to that in a moment. But first we must look at one of the most popular, yet time consuming forms of marketing today. The website. Optimising your website so it appears on the first page of Google is expensive and resource intensive. Achieving first page rankings takes hours and hours of work and a detailed understanding of SEO techniques, keyword strategies and high-quality link building methods.

With the internet, the whole experience of searching for what we need has changed. Whether you are looking for somewhere to eat out, an activity for the weekend or perhaps a local dentist, the internet is probably the first place you'll look. Customers no longer consult the Yellow Pages or the telephone directory to find these places. They're actively using social media and search engines, following up on recommendations and then proceeding to research different options before they make a final decision.

Business owners need to understand the different ways that customers are using online sources to find information about products and services. While a business owner may naturally look for the most effective ways to be in front of their target audience as often as they can, many are not targeting the right places. A marketing strategy needs to be tailored to the needs of the customer and designed to constantly feed the target audience with relevant and tailored content that either addresses a pain point or adds value in some way. With this in mind, what's the one thing that 99% of people in first world countries have on them at all times that will help businesses achieve this? Mobile phones. Everywhere you look, everywhere you go, people are browsing, chatting or sharing information using mobile devices. Many people use their smartphones to access multiple social media accounts every day, so what better way to reach people than through social media marketing? Mobile technology is fueling customers' ability to connect anywhere and everywhere, recieving the latest information in an instant. Consumers are increasingly using their smartphones, tablets and mobile devices to research businesses, compare products and make informed buying decisions. A significant amount of this research is carried out on social media.

The largest social media platform in the world is Facebook, with over 2 billion active users a day as of 2018. As business owners begin to realise the potential of Facebook, they create Facebook pages in the hopes they'll get in front of their target audience. This worked great until 2012 when Facebook changed their algorithm. Organic reach plummeted, and many businesses didn't know what to do. Business pages using organic methods were only reaching between 1 and 3% of their followers, so the chances of being seen reduced substantially. To this day, 99% of companies continue to publish content to Facebook in the hope that it will reach the majority of their followers. They aren't aware that organic reach is so low. As a result, businesses think that social media doesn't work and often give up their social strategy entirely.

Facebook changed their algorithm to obliterate organic reach and to drive businesses towards their paid advertising platform. Facebook advertising is arguably the most powerful platform on the internet today with excellent targeting capabilities, allowing you to drill down into very specific demographics. As an example, if you wished, you could target an ad campaign at women, aged 43 years who live in a certain street in Bulgaria, own a cat and have a love of red jumpers. It's that specific. Using this powerful platform, you can reach ultra targeted audiences for a very small amount of money. But that's not all. As Facebook now own the second largest social media platform, Instagram, you have access to all of their users too.

One of the main issues business owners face is that A, they don't know how to use Facebook Ads properly and B, they don't have the time. That's where social media marketers come in.

A social media marketer will take over the full management of a business' social media page and their paid advertisements. Helping businesses to build a large online presense and ultimately generate a ton of extra revenue per month. Business' are willing to pay thousands for social media marketers. Now, I know what you're thinking, and I thought the same when I first started. Why on earth would a business pay thousands for someone else to manage their social media? Let me explain. Earlier this year, using the techniques and strategies you will learn in this book, I generated 1,350 first time customers in one month for one of my restaurant clients. Let's say the average person spends £20. That's a potential of £27,000 in extra revenue over a single month. This doesn't even take into account that many of these new customers will return themselves but also that they will recommend the restaurant to friends, family and colleagues. It's like a snowball effect. Now just to be clear, we were having a great couple of months with them, but even if I had generated a quarter of that amount of customers, this would still be worth it for them. It's not just large companies you'll be reaching out to either. Actually, the bulk of your client base will be medium sized brick and mortar companies but the value that you can bring to them is huge.

Now I know what you're thinking: How on earth am I going to get results for clients when I have absolutely no marketing experience whatsoever? Well, neither did I. When I first started, I was a complete beginner. I had never created an advert in my life, but I read books, I took courses, I watched YouTube videos and I tested out different methods until I found specific strategies which got ridiculous results and were so easy to implement that absolutely anybody could manage them.

All over the world right now, there are people just like you of all ages making five, six and even seven figure profits from running successful social media agencies. In just a few months you could be following in their footsteps. The majority of those who have taken action and invested in themselves to study this material have had no prior marketing experience and no prior business knowledge. Dispite this, many of them are now managing hugely successful social media businesses from their own home. Some have even built small teams to limit their working hours to just a few a week. Start today. Create the life that you want to live. Travel, spend quality time with your family, follow a dream that you have always wanted and finally live life on your terms. Ready?

Let's get started.

# Stage 1:

---

## How To Get Started, Even If You've Got A Full Time Job Or Are In Full Time Education

# What Companies To Look For And Where To Find Them

All businesses are suitable for social media marketing. Every company needs to market themselves or they'll fall under the shadow of others. When I first started, I would reach out to every single business I could get my hands on, but I quickly realised there were certain industries (niches) that are more profitable and easier to get results for, such as dentists. Dental health is essential; everybody needs to visit a dentist in order to maintain good oral health (or at least they certainly should do). This makes it easy to market for dentists, because the target audience is very large. The same goes for restaurants: everybody needs to eat. In fact, food is a commodity. How many times have you seen an advert with some sexy food on it and instantly felt hungry? It's a marketer's paradise.

To make your lives easier, after much trial and error, I've listed a few perfect starter niches (in no particular order):

- Dentists
- Restaurants
- Gyms
- E-Commerce
- High-End Salons
- Real Estate

It doesn't really matter what niche you choose because the strategies that I will teach you will work in any of the above niches & 95% of others for that matter. Choose those you feel most comfortable with or that interest you the most. Now you know what niches to target, you need to understand how to prospect. What is prospecting? It's the process of finding potential clients - businesses that you can reach out to and ultimately, sign up.

You need to know where to look, who to look for and how to record them (storing their information). There are quite specific pieces of information that you will need to collect which I will share with you in just a second. But first, where exactly do you look for prospects? Well, being in social media marketing, the most obvious place to look would be social media, so we want to utilise the most popular platform - Facebook. All you need to do, is head over to Facebook, go to your search bar and search for the niche in your area.

Now you don't just have to use Facebook. You can use Google, you can use LinkedIn, or you can simply use your local knowledge because you know what companies exist in your local area.

When you're first starting out, you want to look for single location businesses. Why? Because the owner usually works there and when we start reaching out to these businesses, we're much more likely to get through to the right person. If you're reaching out to chains, things can get a little messy and you'll find you're constantly spending time chasing the business owner, depending on where they're located on any given day.

You will also want to reach out to higher-end businesses, to ensure that they can afford your service. For example, if you're reaching out to restaurants, you should target companies who have an average spend per head of at least £20.

When prospecting, it's important that you have a system in place for recording data. You can of course write down the list of all your potential customers, all the businesses that you can reach out to, but this would get messy very quickly. The easiest way would be to put together a simple spreadsheet and use it as a sales database. If you find a business that might be a good fit, create a spreadsheet and add it to your list.

## How To Secure Meetings In Less Than 5 Minutes

You've just put together a list of all your potential clients and you need to start reaching out to them, so how can we make first contact? We can utilise cold calling, door-to-door, emailing or even social media outreach. When I first started, I didn't think I had much time because I was working 9am - 5pm, so I just sent out loads of emails to my whole sales database and got only three responses. Two of them being outright no's. In fact, I didn't manage to convert any meetings from my initial email blast, which was very discouraging. So, I wanted to try something else.

Before my job at the time, I had worked in a call centre, so that was the obvious next step. The thing is... what do you think's going to happen if you call a business owner that's never spoken to you before and the first thing you start doing is pitching to them? Well that's exactly what I did. I thought because I had hard sales experience, that I could adopt the same techniques and pitch over the phone. That didn't exactly go to plan. On my first few call sessions, I wasn't given the time of day and I failed miserably. In fact, one owner even told me to "f*ck off".

It became very clear that these local business owners didn't like direct salesmen, because they get pitches on so many different services every single day. So I threw out all of my corporate sales techniques and went right back to basics. The new purpose for my initial contact was not to pitch my service, but to book in 15 to 30 minutes where I could visit the business and sit down with the owner for a chat.

I started calling my list in the evening on my way home from work, I also booked a holiday day off so I could dedicate it to using this new strategy. In my first few days of trying I set two meetings and managed to convert them into my first two clients, which enabled me to quit my job.

I realised that the most important thing about cold calling is tone. Your tone of voice is the only tool you have when speaking to someone over the phone. As we've already established, these businesses get multiple calls a day and to overcome this, we need to ensure we defuse whoever answers straight away. The chances of the business owner answering the main phone line are pretty slim, you're likely to get through to a receptionist or other member of staff. These are called 'The Gatekeeper'.

The Gatekeeper can be your best friend and your worst enemy. Quite simply, never upset the gatekeeper because they have the power to ensure you never get through to the business owner. There are 3 key rules for getting them to hand the phone over to the owner - be brief, be polite and be important. You need to get straight to the point, ask for the business owner by first name and speak in a clear, confident manner. You should sound like you already know them. **"Hi, can I speak to John please?"** will always have more success than **"Hi can I speak to Mr Smith?"**. There will of course be some cases where you can't find the business owners name, and you'll have to settle for 'the owner' - this is a last resort.

In response to your initial request, the gatekeeper will respond in one of three ways - **"Sure, no problem"**, **"They're not in today"** or **"Can I ask what it's regarding?"**. In the instance that they're not in, simply ask for a time to call back and take a direct email address for future reference (If you don't already have one). If the gatekeeper asks what the call is regarding, state **"I can help you get more customers, I'm not trying to sell anything over the phone don't worry (make humour out of this part)"** - this again ensures you're getting straight to the point, defusing the sales element without having to give away too much information, which again cements that the call is important.

Once you're through to the owner, you'll need to defuse them as well. The best way to do this is by letting them know that you're not going to waste their time. The first thing you want to say is **"Hi John, my name's Jordan. I know you're busy, so am I so I'll be quick"**. This defuses the owner's fears that they're about to get stuck on the phone to a salesman for 20 minutes and by stating the fact that you're busy too, you assert authority over the phone and will earn instant respect. You're then free to move into the reason for your call - **"I help restaurants (or other niche) get more customers through social media marketing and I'm looking to take on 2 new clients this month. I was doing some research the other**

**day and I can see you're leaving a lot of money on the table. So, I'd like to arrange a time when I can come in for 15-20 minutes and share some ideas with you. Sound good?"**. There are a couple of key areas to point out here - firstly, we're specifically stating that we are there to help a certain niche get more clients. This gives us much more credibility and gives the call a personal touch. We're also stating we're only looking to take on 2 new clients this month which implies our service is exclusive and makes the owner feel like they're missing out on something. By stating the business is leaving money on the table, we're resonating with the reason the company was founded in the first place - to make money. Finally, we're making our intentions clear and laying our cards on the table, asking for a meeting.

From here, there are a few possible responses - **"Sounds great"**, **"I'm not interested"** or **"We've already got someone running our social media"**. If they're interested, then you can proceed to book the meeting in for as soon as possible, whilst still allowing yourself a day or two to prepare. If they've stated they're not interested, push back and find out why. If they say they've already got someone running their social media, you can respond with the following **"I know, that's the main reason I called, because I can see you're actively trying at the moment, which is great but you're leaving thousands on the table with your current strategy. I just want to come in and share some ideas with you, no obligations, what have you got to lose?"**. Lots of the time, businesses will already be posting on social media and not getting any results, this is because as we covered at the start of this book, Facebook's algorithm means that only 1-2% of the people who like a page actually see the posts. Companies often just assume that Facebook doesn't work, although in reality, it's because they're barely touching the tip of the iceberg. By acknowledging the fact that they're already trying, we overcome this rejection and confirm that we have a lot of value to add to their business. **"What have you got to lose?"** is also a very powerful statement, as it makes the owner question themselves and see reason.

In summary, cold calling when done right is without a doubt the most effective way to secure meetings. It's how I secured 99% of mine at the start of my journey.

For extended learning on Stage 1, visit:
www.15minuteagency.com/learnmore/1

# Stage 2:

---

## How To Sign Your First 4 Figure Deal In Just 15 Minutes

# You're Not 'Selling' A Thing

When I had secured my first meeting, I had such a cocky mindset, as if I was the king of sales. I remember thinking to myself "this will be a walk in the park. I'm going to breeze it". The morning of the meeting I had all these corporate sales techniques in my mind. I walked in the door and went all guns blazing, laying absolutely all of my cards on the table within about 5 minutes... and I'd never seen someone look so uninterested in my life. The owner called a break, so she could go make a cup of coffee and I remember sitting there dwelling on what I was doing wrong.

I then had a realisation, I didn't need to 'sell' to this business owner at all. They had already pre-sold themselves when they accepted a meeting with me. They agreed to a meeting because they acknowledge the fact that they can and should be making more money per month, which means they also acknowledge that there are problems within their business which are causing those money voids. So, I decided to take a step back and treat the meeting for exactly what it was - one business owner having a coffee with another, one hoping that the other can be the **solution** to the problems they're facing.

When she got back from making us coffee, I completely changed my tone. I was more relaxed, I completely ditched the 'salesy' approach and simply started to have a conversation. We spoke in-depth about the business, her ambitions, what's working well, what's not working and suddenly she unloaded all of these problems. It was like a weight lifted off her shoulder. As she listed these issues, I scribbled them down on my note pad and tried to think of solutions in my head... solutions that I could use as fuel later on in the meeting. Long story short, by some kind of miracle, I completely transformed the direction of the meeting and managed to sign her up. That was my first ever client and if you were a fly on the wall watching the first half, you would have given me no chance of closing them. This is why building a rapport with prospects is so important.

The craziest thing of all is I realised that my sales experience was completely irrelevant. Once you strip the meeting back and treat it as a **conversational problem solving exercise,** you realise absolutely anybody can do it. You're simply having a conversation with someone about their problems. You do this on a daily basis already, I bet you moan to your friends and family about other people or your job or something you're not happy with. We all moan. We all have problems and we're always looking for solutions for those problems. We are the solution to these business owners' problems. Business owners all share a common trait - passion. They're so passionate about their business and the problems they're facing that when you start to show them potential solutions or at least talk about solutions, you don't even have to sell.

When I got home from closing my first client, I was so inspired about my realisation that I put together a 3-stage system for me to follow in all of my future meetings, a system which now has enabled me to sign multiple 6 figures worth of business. What are these stages? Discover, Present and Close. Let's dive into each of these in greater detail.

# Part 1 - Discover

The discovery stage of the meeting strategy is all about taking control and learning as much as possible about the potential client, so we can use the information as fuel later in the meeting. In his book, How to Win Friends and Influence People, Dale Carnegie emphasized the importance of making other people feel important and this is exactly what you will do in the discovery process. Make the business owner feel that they are important, and their future success is also important to you.

Before you dive straight into interrogating the owner, you need to ask yourself - Are you going to take control of the meeting or is the meeting going to take control of you? In any kind of meeting, no matter what the industry, someone must be in control and that always has to be the person 'selling' or else you'll struggle to build enough credibility and ultimately will fail.

Taking control starts before you walk through the door, it begins with your mindset. It's important for you to become an alpha. Before you enter, you need to remind yourself of what you're actually doing for this business. You're meeting this business owner because you can make *them* thousands of extra revenue per month. Money that they weren't making before they met you. That means that they need you. It instantly makes you valuable and as such, you need to lift yourself with that thought and understand your self value. Elevate yourself, because you can do something for this business that they can't do by themselves. Your job is to show them how you can help transform their business, helping them move from where they are now to where they want to be.

So, you're now psyched up... you're in alpha mode and you've just walked through the door, shaken hands with the owner and sat down ready to get cracking. Before we jump into taking control, it's important to have a little small talk. Discuss the weather, sport, how their weeks been, what you had for tea last night... no, seriously, just break the ice and make simple conversation. If you're really stuck on this, the weather and the events of your day are usually good places to begin.

Once you've got the awkward small talk out of the way, you're going to throw something controversial in the mix and this will throw the owner off completely. Simply ask **"So why did you invite me in today?"** - This little question is so powerful, because we all know that we cold called the business, but the owner actively agreed to a meeting and there is a reason behind this that we want to dig up. This reason is the key to us signing the client.

At this stage, the owner is going to be thinking something along the lines of *"Ok, well they called me but technically I did invite them in... because I'm not earning enough money, or this isn't selling well. Tuesdays aren't busy enough"* - it's making them question themselves and it puts you in the dominant position, right from the very start of the meeting.

We'll then further cement our dominance by explaining how you expect the meeting to go - **"I want to start this meeting by having a conversation about your business. I need to understand your current position and some of the problems you're facing before I can show you how I can help, as my service is completely bespoke."** - It's in a business owners' nature to want to take control but by laying our cards on the table we make it crystal clear to the owner that we're going to lead the meeting. This will also prevent them from butting in to change the direction at any point.

On that note, don't be afraid to stand your ground and more importantly, always follow the plan. The last thing you want is an owner trying to throw your plan out of the window. Try to avoid reinventing the wheel or deviating too far from the scripts that I have shown you. On my 4th meeting, I met with a local Gym owner and only 10 minutes in he stated, *"Can we just get straight to it, how much do you charge?"* - the worst thing I could have done here was skip to presenting my costs, I would have built zero credibility and there would of been absolutely zero chance of signing the client. Instead I stood firm, stating **"I approached you because I can see you're leaving money on the table, although I don't work with any business, I arranged this meeting to see if we're a good fit for each other. Before we can talk about pricing, I need to learn more about your business, as my service is completely bespoke. There is no one size fits all with social media marketing."**

Just like we said in the initial cold call and rightly so, there is no one size fits all with social media marketing and by standing firm and stating this, you'll gain instant respect and take back control. In that counter-statement, I also reconfirmed the structure of the meeting. Now there will be rare occasions when you meet with a particularly stubborn business owner who won't stop trying to dominate the meeting, speaking over you, changing the conversation and just generally being a nuisance... in this instance, don't think twice to cut the meeting short - these are the businesses you want to avoid, if you can't have a simple first meeting, imagine what they would be like if you managed to sign them up!

So just to recap, you need to be an alpha, take control, stand your ground and always follow the plan. Now we're going to jump into some discovery questions. As we established earlier, we want to learn as much as possible about the business, so we have ammunition for later on in the meeting. We need to learn about their ambitions, what sells well, what doesn't sell well, busy days, quiet days and even their financial situation. In doing this we're not just getting ammunition, we're also establishing whether the client is actually suitable for us. If we get the impression that the owner has lost love, motivation and no longer cares about the development of their business, then there's no point us working with them, they'd be a hopeless client. We also want to make sure the problems they're facing are actually solvable with our service. We're not miracle workers, if a restaurant isn't getting clients because their food is terrible, we can't fix that with social media.

To kick start our discovery questions, straight after taking control of the meeting ask, **"Can you show me an example of your current digital marketing strategy?"** - this will completely throw them off. You need to ask like you're just presuming they already have one, but I can almost guarantee you they won't. They'll be thinking *"Sh*t, I haven't got a digital marketing strategy... I obviously should have one"*. You've now got them on the back foot, they've just told you they don't have one, you should then fire back with **"Ok, well what systems do you have in place to get new customers?" -** this is when you'll get the most info, they'll probably list off a number of different ways they advertise their business - newspaper ads, billboards, flyers etc. After they've finished explaining, say **"Ok, do you know how much money you're leaving on the table by not having a digital marketing strategy?" -** This statement should be lighthearted, you should almost make a joke out of it, it'll again make them question if they've been missing out, if they've been doing something wrong all this time.

We've just broken down some walls and established that there is room for our service, now we need to find out the specifics. Ask the below questions, scribbling down each answer as you go along, you don't have to ask them in any particular order and you can throw others into the mix too, just make sure it's conversational and not like an interrogation session.

**"What do you sell well on?" / "What doesn't sell well?" - "Why do you think this is?"**

**"What days you busy on?" / "What days aren't so busy?" - "Why do you think this is?"**

These questions force the owner to think about all the problems they've been brushing under the carpet. All businesses have days they're busy and days when they're not so busy on, services that sell well and services that don't sell well. By asking these questions they'll start questioning why they have these problems. After we've discussed, ask **"What's stopping you from solving these issues on your own?" -** this will make them realise that they cannot solve the problems by themselves, or they would have already done so. Generally, it's going to come down to either time or knowledge but regardless of their answer, we're starting to get some self-acceptance of issues. Now, we need to learn about the financials, ask **"What's your average price per customer?" -** We need to know this so later on we can work out how many customers we need to bring them in order to obtain an acceptable ROI. We then want to ask, **"What are your average monthly revenue figures?"** - Again, to be used as fuel later in the meeting. This is the only question that you can face rejection on, some businesses are hesitant to disclose revenue, although always push back with **"It's important that I understand the ins and outs of your business. I'm a results based marketer, my number one priority is making you money and in order to do that effectively, I need to understand where you're at financially. This conversation is completely confidential, in fact I'm more than happy to sign a non-disclosure agreement."** - 99% of the time the owner will then happily discuss figures. Once they do discuss figures, you'll reach a new level of trust and buy-in, making it a lot easier to be transparent and up-front for the rest of the meeting.

Once we know some specifics about their current situation, we want to try and ignite a spark within them, the spark that lead to them launching their business in the first place... that burning hunger to succeed. At the end of the day, hunger for success is what links all of us businesspeople together. Whilst you're reading this thinking about your vision of a six or seven figure marketing agency, Joe Blogs down the road who owns Blog's Steakhouse has a vision too. When he launched that business, I'm sure he aspired to have his steakhouse on every street in his city. He knew where he wanted to take the business and had no doubt spent hours on financial plans for when he reached his summit. With that in mind, ask **"Where would you like to take your business and what should your revenue figures be if all the discussed problems were solved?"** - This will take them back to the business' infancy and hopefully act as a reminder that they're not currently where they want to be, motivating them to make a change. *Make sure to write down the answers to* *this question as they can be used as powerful pain-points later on.*

At this point, we've created a mindset shift. You're making them think *"Maybe I am leaving money on the table. This isn't okay. I have got complacent. I do need to make a difference and perhaps this person is the key, this person might actually be able to change all of this"* - you're changing your image from salesperson to someone who genuinely cares and wants to help. This is why the discovery stage is so crucial to a meetings success, as there are many barriers to be broken. Don't be afraid of getting personal, let the conversation go off on tangents, let it flow naturally but always bring it back to the basic structure I'm outlining for you and if it makes you feel more confident, you can even write down your list of questions on a notepad and bring it along.

## Building Buy-In

Now we've learnt more about the inner workings of the business, we need to emotionally tie everything up and create buy-in. We've already ignited their entrepreneurial spark but now we need to make it achievable. We need to close the gap.

What do I mean by closing the gap? Put simply, the gap is the difference between a current situation and a desired situation. In this instance, the businesses current revenue vs desired revenue. To kick this off, grab a piece of paper from your notebook and write down the letter A on the left hand side, circle it and write their current monthly revenue next to it. Say **"So, this is where you're at currently" (see below example £20,000)**

Then, on the right hand side, write the letter C, circle it write their 'should be' revenue if all their current problems were solved. Explaining **"and, this is where you should be, if all your current issues were resolved *proceed to list issues that you just wrote**

**down*" (see below example £50,000)**

Finally, explain **"So this is where you are and where you should be, but let's be realistic here, we both know these things can't be resolved overnight"**. Proceed to then write a letter B in the centre of the page, circle it and ask them **"Where should we be realistically, if we can begin to resolve the problems?" -** It's important that you come up with this figure collectively and if the business owner dictates it themselves, it's even better! Doing this, instead of going straight down the middle, will create instant buy-in from the business.

Now, we need to emotionally attach them to the attractive new financial figures you've just discussed. We need them to envisage how life would be if they were bringing in X amount extra every month. Ask them **"How would you feel if you were at point B, or even C? How would it impact your personal life?" "Would you get more time?" -** You don't need to ask these questions word for word, it's more important that the conversation flows and at this point, you're allowing the owner to speak and share their thoughts. We need them to picture their life having reached a new financial level within their business and we need them to picture how that would impact them, whether that means more time to spend with their kids, wife or even more cashflow to spend on material things. Regardless of this, it'll make them attached to the idea of achieving it.

As important as it is to plant the seed of success, we also need to plant the seed of failure. Once you've finished talking about the positive impact of higher earnings, flip the scenario and ask **"How would you feel if the gap was never closed? If you never reached point C and stayed at point A?"** In asking this after we've fed them a taste of success, they'll self-acknowledge that they're not content with the current state of their business. You'll have them bought into the idea that they need someone else to help them reach this point. We need to further cement by stating **"I understand your problems and I know how we can solve them, would you like me to show you how we can begin to close the gap?"** - This further reassures that we know how to solve their problems and also opens the conversation for a smooth transition onto presenting our services. In order to make the transition, explain **"Great, I've prepared a simple presentation for you, let's move on to the next step."**

## Recap

The discovery stage is all about learning as much as we can about the business. We want to know the ins and outs of the businesses, so we can begin to understand the issues they're facing, such as the days they're busy on, what days they're not so busy on, what sells well, what doesn't sell well, and you can use all of this as fuel throughout the meeting.

By asking questions such as **"Where would you like to take your business and what should your revenue be if these problems were solved?"**, you're igniting a spark in their brain. Again, you're making them think about how they used to feel when they started that business, when they had vision and hunger, like you right now, you may be thinking - *"I want to earn seven figures one day"*, *"I want to earn seven figures"*, *"I want to take my life to the next level"* ... all business owners do the same. Business owners want money and that's the reason why we all start in the first place, whatever money means to you, whether that's freedom to spend time with your family or even just to buy nice things, it's what we all have in common. So, by asking these questions, you're really igniting that spark in their brain by asking them **"Do you know how much money you're leaving on the table?"**.

We're then diving even further and throwing emotions into the mix by closing the gap and painting a picture for them. You're establishing an emotional connection with these financial figures. Making them realise that point A isn't where they want to be anymore. That's not what they want. That's not where they should be. They should be at point C. At the very least they should be reaching point or striving toward it B. We're asking about the impact on their personal life and their business life and really understanding what it would mean to them. You're then going to bring it all back to earth and ask how it would feel if they never progressed any further, giving that final push to acknowledge that you're the key they need to reach the level they want to reach. This is an important step in the process and it leads on nicely to the next step in the process; presenting your services.

# Part 2 - Present

In this part of the strategy, we'll be laying all of our cards on the table and showing the business owner exactly what we can offer them. By the end of it, our service is going to be so desirable that saying no isn't even going to be an option. Our biggest tool throughout this whole section are the 3 Weapons of Influence, inspired by Robert Cialdini's Six Principles of Influence featured in his best selling book Influence: The Psychology of Persuasion. So, what are they?

Let's start with The Law of Social Proof. People are influenced by others, that's no hidden fact and this is particularly apparent on social media. Let's look at Kim Kardashian as an example. If Kim wears a certain brand of make up or buys a certain brand of shoe. Every woman following her wants that makeup, or those shoes. They're so influenced by her as a figure, that they instantly trust any product that she may use. They don't need to be persuaded to buy something, the social proof is all they need to make a buying decision. It's clear to see why she has been paid up to $500,000 by companies for a single Instagram post. Kim Kardashian's name associated with a brand is a powerful statement and is enough to result in thousands of purchases. That being said, it's not just celebrities that have this influence. Everyday people, consumers, colleagues, friends, family and businesses have this power too. Let's take restaurants as an example. If I'm looking for a restaurant in my local city and I stumble across a Facebook page and they've got lots of positive comments on every picture stating how good the food is I'm going to automatically think of this as a great restaurant and a place that I should visit. I'll think *"Well, if everyone else is loving it, it must be good"* - Just by law of social proof.

Secondly, we have The Law of Comparison. It's in human nature to hate being compared to others, it's never pleasant to be told that someone is better than you. More often than not, it leads to insecurity and with insecurity, comes a desire to change. The principle is the same with business. If you were to compare a business owner to another business owner, especially if it's one of their direct competitors, it'll create doubt, insecurity and again, a desire to change. In this instance, we'll be comparing the social media posts of competitors in the hopes to ignite a competitive spark and a determination to do better.

Finally, The Law of Authority. When you convey yourself as an authority figure, someone who can demonstrate that you know what you're talking about, this creates trust. Authority will be built throughout your presentation to the client because you will be providing a huge amount of value. You won't just be telling them you will be showing them how what you can offer will help them reach their goals and solve their problems. As you deliver your presentation you will gain respect with your prospect by teaching them what you know. Ultimately, you will be the marketing expert because you will have the tools and know-how to transform businesses. Not only will you know the ins and outs of social media marketing, you will be able to educate your prospect on the top strategies they need to implement to achieve a consistent return on investment. By implementing your strategies, the businesses will be able to generate thousands in extra revenue per month. How do we do this? Well we need to give them some free value by specifically showing them how a Facebook advertisement works. You will guide the prospect through each stage in Facebook advertising, discussing the algorithm, the mechanics of paid ads, and just how detailed Facebook targeting can be. By using the law of authority, you will build all the trust and credibility required to get the client signed up on the spot.

Now you understand the 3 Weapons of Influence, let's get started on the presentation. Before we begin, it is important to remember that a presentation must be polished and delivered with poise and professionalism. How you deliver this presentation is completely up to you. Personally, I'm a lover of keeping everything as informal and relaxed as possible, instead of using in-depth slideshows. In fact, I simply talk through a series of screenshots on my tablet. It's quick, easy and means you can travel light but by all means, a laptop is perfectly suitable. On my first ever meeting, I didn't have access to either, so I printed these screenshots on paper, which didn't hinder my results at all. So, don't over think this part.

The first screenshot is simply going to be their Facebook page **(Figure 1)**. We're going to provide some free advice and serve up a delicious 'sh*t sandwich'. This is simply a technique used for critiquing someone without being offensive, essentially complimenting (bread), criticising (sh*t) and complimenting (bread) again.

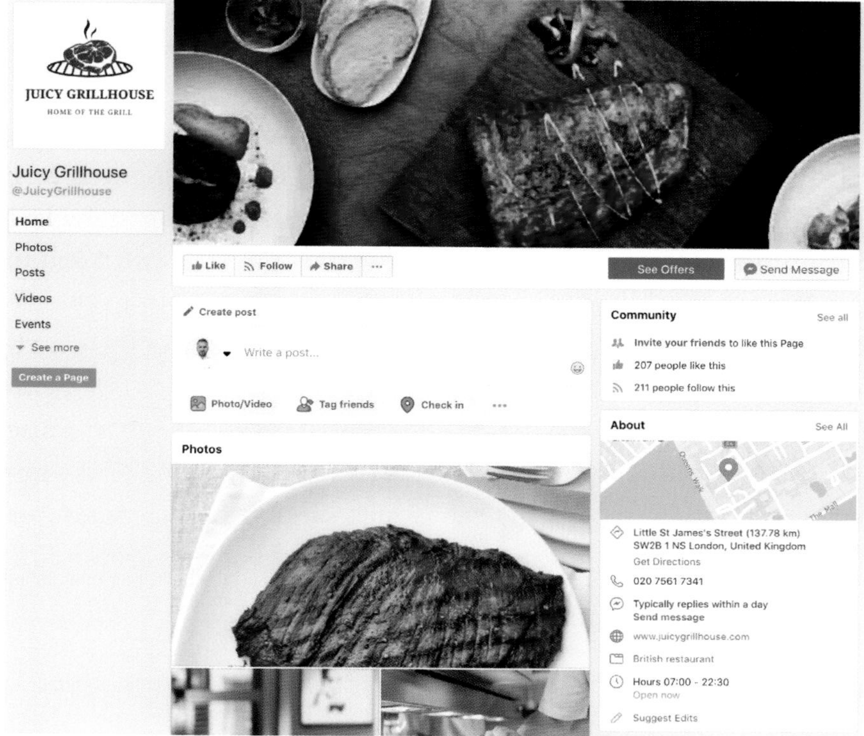


Fig. 1: Screenshot of clients Facebook Page

Using the above example, I could say something along the lines of **"As you can see, this is a screenshot of your Facebook page. Firstly, you've got a nice clean logo and a great base of likes on here too. But your cover photo is pixelated currently which paints a poor image of you and you're also completely missing Facebook recommendations which are extremely powerful for restaurants, you're leaving money on the table without having those. Currently, your customers will have to visit external websites to see what others have to say about**

**your food and service, although if you had it right on your page, you'd convert a ton more visitors into customers."** – This exact script will let them down gently without offending them and although the compliments will be a temporary high for them, the criticism will stick. We then need to hit them with a final bit of reassurance, the last slice of bread and state **"Overall though, you have the perfect base for my service and I know I can do a lot for you"** - you're going to say this to everyone but because if you've done your prospecting correctly, you'll already know that they're the perfect potential client.

Moving on to screenshot number two **(Figure 2)**, we're going show them one or two of their posts (preferably a post with poor engagement) and adopt the same 'sh*t sandwich' technique. We will compliment, critique and discuss the Facebook algorithm.

Fig. 2: Screenshot of clients Facebook post

I would say something like **"Here's one of your recent posts, firstly, that burger looks incredible I could eat it right now, it's making me hungry! Your text isn't bad either, although the**

**hashtags you've used are unnecessary as nobody will be searching for #Juicy or #Tasty on Facebook. The biggest problem though, is that you have very poor engagement, even though you've got a great deal to shout about. You should be achieving a higher response rate than this but unfortunately you have a very small number of likes. The low engagement and response rate is not because you need to produce better content, it's simply because of the Facebook algorithm. It all goes back to their 2012 algorithm change where organic posts now only reach between 2% and 3% of your followers. Facebook did this because they wanted to push users towards their paid advertising platform."** In doing this, we eliminate any doubts that they may have about Facebook. Like most business owners who don't understand the algorithm, they probably just thought Facebook doesn't work. By teaching them this, you're gaining their trust and their buy-in. It's very important that you always discuss Facebook's algorithm in this way, whilst talking through one of their posts. It's a very simple move that will place you at a huge advantage.

Using the current example, I would also highlight the fact that this post would be perfect for an advert and is in fact wasted as an organic post, stating **"Another thing to mention, the purpose of this post was to get people in for your £9.99 burgers, right? Well, this post would actually be perfect for an advert. We can create an ad which would allow people to redeem the offer through Facebook, which they can then show to your team on arrival. This would be a very effective strategy for this particular offer" -** It's always good, where possible to try doing this, so be mindful of it whilst selecting one of your potential client's posts to use during your meeting. This is just another way that you can add value and build that all important authority.

Now onto screenshot number three **(Figure 3)**. In this example, we are going to compare our potential client to one of their competitors, using the Law of Comparison. Firstly, you'll need to search for businesses in the same industry in the same area (go for the big ones) and click the 'info and ads' button on their Facebook page. This is the page that shows all adverts a page is currently running. Click on some of the ads until you find one with lots of engagement. Alternatively, if you can't find any direct competitors who are currently running ads, you can look further afield. Number of engagements doesn't matter so much, as long as it's a fair bit better than your potential client.

Fig. 3: Screenshot of competitors Facebook post

We're now going to adopt a slightly different tactic and throw out the second slice of bread. We'll complement and then we'll critique. Using this post as an example **"Ok, so this is one of Steak and Grill's posts which has been set up as an advert. It's got 266 likes and tons of comments, the majority of which are tagging their friends and family stating that they'd like to visit the restaurant. So, there are a ton of potential customers on this post but even more than that, imagine what kind of impression this post leaves on new page visitors too, when they see all these other people raving about how amazing the food looks or is. It's excellent social proof. If for instance I was looking on Facebook for a restaurant to visit and I'd visited both of your pages, it would be a clear decision for me. Despite all of this though, it's a very standard photograph and actually yours looks far more attractive. Can you imagine how well your post would perform if we published it as an ad?" -** At this stage we want our potential client to be intimidated by their competitors post but at the same time we finish by complimenting their post again, assuring them that theirs could be even better. This will make them feel very competitive.

So, we've now gone through the visuals and why ads are important, now we're going to walk the client through how it all works. To transition this, say something like **"Ok so let me show you how adverts are made and the specific types of ad that we can actually create."** - This part will include 3 screenshots, starting with a general screenshot of Facebook's campaign selection page **(Figure 4).** Don't worry if you've never seen this page before, It'll be second nature to you once I teach you about ads later.

What's your marketing objective? Help: Choosing an objective

| Awareness | Consideration | Conversion |
| --- | --- | --- |
| Brand Awareness | Traffic | Conversions |
| Reach | Engagement | Catalogue Sales |
| | App Installs | Store Visits |
| | Video Views | |
| | Lead Generation | |
| | Messages | |

Fig. 4: Screenshot of Facebook ad objective page

When you're creating a new advert, these are the objective options you have. You're essentially being asked what it is you're trying to achieve from your adverts - brand awareness, reach, web traffic, catalog sales if you sell online, lead generation and more. There are three main objectives that we'll focus on across the majority of our clients - Traffic, Engagement and Video Views. To explain these to the client, state **"This is the campaign creation page of Facebook advertising, where you select a clear objective for your advert, whatever that may be. Generally, I focus on traffic, engagement and video ads"** And you're going to teach them about those different ad objectives. For example, **"Ok so Traffic ads. They're pretty self-explanatory, we're aiming to drive traffic from A to B. In this instance it's from your Facebook page to whatever website you would like."** Depending on the client it may be a landing page, their blog, a product page or a signup form. Then give an example relevant to their business such as **"For you it would probably be your Facebook page straight to your booking page, so people can make reservations online."**

**"Then we have engagement. Engagement is such an important metric because it represents all of the likes, comments and shares associated with your post(s). Using the content of your post, Facebook will directly target people who are likely to engage with your post. This is excellent for creating social proof, just like what I showed you from Steak and Grill. Video views are very similar to this, although they are tailored to getting as many video watches as possible. This is excellent for brand awareness campaigns. If we get a video of some really tasty food, of your chef cooking, maybe even some happy customers as well, we could then create a video views ad and get it in front of everyone in the city."**

Now you've covered the different ad objectives, we're going to show them how in-depth Facebook's targeting system is. We'll pull up a screenshot of the targeting options **(Figure 5)**. You'll always want this to be a traffic advert. Simply select traffic on the campaign objection page and input some relevant targeting to your potential client. Now, I realise that some of you will not have seen this page either, but as I said a moment ago, it'll be second nature to you soon, so don't feel daunted about something that is actually ridiculously easy once you know how. Targeting wise, be sure to input their address, so in this instance it's Park St James in London and I have inputted a five kilometer radius around that area. If it was a more rural area, I'd probably put around 20 kilometers but again we'll go into that later on. You'll also need to set a £5 a day ad spend (or your equivalent currency) and finally, input some simple interest targeting relevant to the business, which can be seen in the below example. This is essentially their ideal audience.

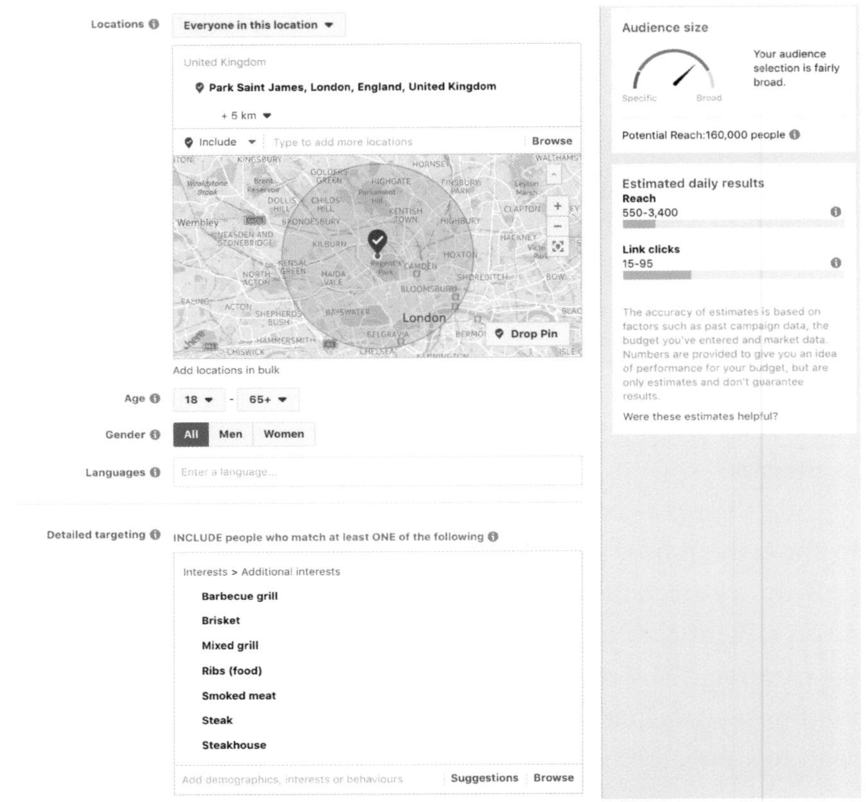


Fig. 5: Screenshot of Facebook ad targeting page

Using the screenshot as an example, we'll discuss how Facebook know all of this information and where they get their data. For example, **"Moving on, this where you select targeting for your ads. Facebook have data sources from all over the world although their biggest source is themselves. They can track every word exchanged, every message sent, every page liked, every restaurant checked-in and over time their algorithm learns about**

**you as an individual. Using this data, if you really wanted to you could target women, aged 43 who live on oxford street, eat sushi and own cats"** - they'll laugh at this because its humorous but it'll also leave a lasting 'wow' because they wouldn't of realised how pin-point targeted Facebook ads can be.

We also need to explain what we've inputted on this specific screen shot, for example **"On this specific example, I've inputted the data of an ideal audience for you. As you can see, I've selected a 5km radius around your restaurant, targeting all age groups who are interested in your cuisine type"**, we also need to discuss the right hand side of the page. Explaining **"If I move you over to the right hand side, this is where Facebook show the size of your selected audience (160,000 people) and also predictions for how well the ad is going to perform based on the data provided. In this instance I've inputted a £5 a day advert spend, which will result in 550-3,400 people a day seeing your ad and 15-95 clicks to wherever we're driving traffic to. That could be your reservations page for example".**

Now we're ready to throw some financials into the mix, using some very quick maths - **"So that's an average of let's say 40 link clicks a day, now even if just 10% of these people were to proceed to make a reservation, that's 4 bookings per day, each of those bringing an average of 2 people with them. That's 12 customers a day at an average spend of £20 each (the figure you discussed in the discovery stage). That's a potential £240 per day, from just a £5 investment. On the basis of only 10% of people proceeding to book. People that have already been warmed up by incredible social proof on your page, from the engagement ads we'll have running too."** - Again, this will wow them and create the ultimate buy-in. This is even more powerful because we've already taught the business owner how it all works, so they understand the mechanics behind ads and what results they can bring too. At this point, they're going to be eating out of the palm of your hand.

To really get them on their knees, once you have your first few clients under your belt, this is the perfect time to further cement your expertise by showing some of the ads you've created before and amazing them with the results. When you're first starting, you'll have no results to show, although don't worry, you simply don't need them. When I first started, I was never once asked for proof of previous results, because the value and authority I built through my presentation created more than enough buy-in.

If on the flip side you do have results to show, screenshot a few ads and walk the client through the monetary ROI's you obtained. This will make light work of ensuring all meetings are a no-brainer close.

## Quick Recap

Overall, the presentation is very, very simple. It's just a conversation over a series of screenshots, using our good friends - the 3 Weapons of Influence. The Law of Social Proof, The Law of Comparison, and The Law of Authority. We'll be serving up 'sh*t sandwiches' all round, discussing their page, their posts, competitors posts and finally moving on to teaching them about ad objectives, targeting, tying everything up with financials and finally, previous results (if you have them). Granted, it's a lot of information for a business owner to take on, so now's a good time to ask if they have any questions and iron out any concerns before you proceed to the next step, the close.

# 3. Close

Welcome to this lesson. We are finally at the end of the meeting strategy. It's part four, the close, getting that big fat yes, that signature on the dotted line, and that chunky pay-check in your bank account every month.

We're finally at the end of the meeting strategy. The close... the *'let's do this'*, signature on the dotted line and last but not least, the pay-check. So, as always, the transition from presentation to close needs to be smooth. To do this, we're going to eliminate any potential concerns, starting with how you can track results through the Facebook advertisement. Now as a business owner, you'd want to be able to track where extra revenue is coming, so they know you're doing your job properly. For example, **"With Facebook ads, you can track every single penny spent and even what spends correspond to specific ads"**. We'll then move onto explain the Facebook Pixel.

Now I understand lots of you reading this right now won't have a clue what the Pixel is. In its most basic form, the Facebook pixel is a bit of code you can install on the header of a website which will enable Facebook to talk to your site and allow us to track all the people coming from Facebook. We can even track what they're specifically doing. Whether they are making bookings, viewing a menu, a product, or any specific page, or signing up to a newsletter. What's great about this is you can run ads which re-target these people. This is also how you would explain it to the business owner.

We can also dive a little deeper into link click tracking, explaining, **"you can even track specifically how much one singular link click is costing you, through the CPC (Cost Per Click) metric. Or, for example, If we were to run a redeemable offer ad, like I mentioned earlier, you'd be able to track exactly how many redemptions were made on specific days" -** this will eliminate any doubts.

So, we've covered how to track financial ROI, but social ROI is just as important. **"We then have the social ROI too, all the likes, the comments, the tags and the shares. Everybody engaging with your posts. It's a snowball effect... if just one person has a good experience in your restaurant they'll tell their family and their friends, who will also recommend the restaurant and so it continues as more and more people visit. Over time the momentum will increase and social ROI both on social media and the real world will continue to stack up organically."**

On that note, it's vitally important that at this stage we manage the expectations of the business owner. For example, **"As with all marketing, it's important to find the right audience as quickly as possible, which is why on the first month, we test a variety of different traffic audiences whilst warming up these audiences with engagement posts, which will generate huge social ROI's. Making you revenue is our utmost priority, hence we start revenue generating ads from day 1. That being said, you're a businessperson, you know Rome wasn't built in a day. It's the 30-90 day point when the profits really start to kick in, once we've found the perfect audience and warmed them up nicely. After then, it's just a matter of scaling up your ad spend until we hit that perfect balance of Ad Spend vs ROI. The biggest beauty of all this is,**

**as you'll be providing such a great service to all these new customers, they'll keep coming back again and again, bringing more people with them and that snowball is going to keep growing larger every single month" -** At this point we should also mention some of the issues we discussed back in the discovery stage, reading back some of our notes, showing that we genuinely care about the businesses problems and further cementing our professionalism. For instance, **"It's also important that we target all of those weak spots we discussed earlier, the fact that Tuesdays are quiet, and steaks don't sell well for example. We'll create bespoke ad strategies to directly overcome those issues"** - never underestimate the power that listening and genuine care can have on your ability to sign clients. This is why it's so important to write down answers during the discovery stage.

We've just ironed out any final worries or concern that a business could have... apart from cost. Now it's time to close. We're going to use a very simple two question close. Firstly **"Do you believe that I understand the issues you are facing as a business?"** So, if you went through the discovery stage correctly, you went through building buy-in, you've learnt about all of the problems that they're facing, the days they're not busy, and the days they are, the products that sell well, the products that don't. You went through closing the gap and emotional tie in. They're going to answer *"Yes, of course"*. It's a no-brainer answer. Secondly, ask **"Do you think I have the skills to help you solve these problems?"** **-** Again, if you've gone through your presentation right, you've shown them their posts, taught them about where they're going wrong, discussed why their competitors are doing well, shown them different ad objectives and gone into targeting options, maybe you already have clients and you've shown them previous results too. Everything that you've done so far in this meeting has been tactically building the fundamentals of trust, authority and buy-in. At this point you'll be respected as someone with great knowledge of social media marketing. Of course, they're going to say yes, because you'll have already filled them with that confidence throughout the meeting.

If for whatever reason they say no to any of these questions, simply ask why and iron out their concern. No business owner will ever get to this point in a meeting, say no and not give you a reason as to why they don't think you have the skills to solve their problems. Once you've answered their concerns, ask the two closing questions again.

What we've just achieved is an acceptance, without discussing price. We've validated to ourselves that they are confident that we understand what needs to be done in order to help them generate more revenue through social media. Once you've got a yes on both questions, state, **"Great, let's take the next step. What is your current marketing budget?" -** It's important to always ask this question because even though 99% of the time they'll say, *"we don't have one" or "non-existent"*, just because they want to get your lowest price. Sometimes you'll come across businesses who are more transparent. I have a student currently (Frantz) who's third ever client told him they had a $350k advert budget. It's the transparent business owners we're hoping for when we ask this, because the larger the ad budget, the more service charge we can demand. Frantz for an example managed to close that client for a healthy

$9,500 monthly service charge.

Ultimately, your service charge depends on the value you can bring to a business. There are many factors which will affect your service charge, and they all boil down to the potential revenue that you can generate through your service. Firstly, look at their current financials, the ABC that we went through in the building buy-in stage. Compare point A to point B, and even point C. This is the gap that we can potentially close if we resolve their current issues. If the gap between A and B is £10,000 or even £5,000, us charging £1,000 is more than reasonable. It would be a no-brainer for them. If the gap is larger, you can charge more. Personally, I think the minimum charge for ad management and daily organic posting on 1 social media platform should be £1,000. It's what I signed my first two clients up for and what I recommend to all of my students. That being said, it's all relative. The last thing you want to do is limit yourself to one thousand. You should always be aiming for more, be it 2k, 5k or even 10k+. It all boils down to value. Take Frantz for example. He had strong self-value and went straight in for the close at $9,500.

Generally, the higher end the business, the higher end the products, the more costly they are, then the more you can charge. The more money you can make a business, the more money you can charge them.

It's not just your service charge that needs to be considered, but the advert budget too. The client always pays the advert budget, never us. Generally, for an average sized brick and mortar business, I advise an absolute minimum spend of £500 per month. Again, this is completely dependent on the nature of the business.

For example an e-commerce business could be spending 10's if not 100's of thousands per month on adverts. The ad budget also needs to be relative to your service charge. We cannot charge £5,000 for service and expect a £500 advert budget. It's not going to be sufficient enough budget to get return on investment and cover the costs of our service. The advert budget needs to be a minimum of 50% our service charge, but ideally 100% or even more. The higher the advert budget, the easier it is for you to get ROI.

Let me tell you something, £1,000 is cheap for this service. We're being paid to transform businesses and not just in revenue, but their whole online brand presence. The power of social media marketing spans far beyond running a few ads and getting a quick ROI. The social impact a good brand can have on the success of a business will last a lifetime.

So, going back to the strategy, we've just asked for their current marketing budget. We're now going to go in with our price summary; for example, **"For full advert management, including the full management of your daily content writing and posting on Facebook (and Instagram or any other platform you agree on), my service charge is £1,000 a month and based on what we've discussed today, my advised starting advert spend is £500" -** It's important to be clear and confident when you discuss price; never hesitate at this point as it will show weakness and a lack of confidence that you can do what you're saying you can.

Once you get that yes, we want to get everything tied up as soon as possible. You don't want to give them the chance to change their mind. Chances are they're not going to change their mind, but with sales, the client is never closed until you have a signature. Respond with **"Excellent, let me put together a contract which will include my marketing proposal, and we'll get started right away. I'll pop in tomorrow, we can get the contract signed, arranged the first month's payment and get your first set of adverts launched?"** - If the client can't do the day after, arrange the nearest day they're free. Alternatively, you can send over an e-contract but you'll still want to arrange a kick-off meeting to talk them through your proposal, potential offers for ads and to tie up any lose ends.

If for whatever reason you don't get an instant yes, make sure you push back and find out the reasons why. The majority of the time you'll be able to overcome these issues. Generally, any objection you'll receive will be due to failures to build enough authority and trust throughout the meeting as an objection is simply a sign of doubt. When you are first starting, it is natural to make mistakes, it's what makes us all human. The key is to not get disheartened and to jump straight back on the horse to secure more meetings.

We're there... the end of the meeting strategy. Like everything, the more you do it, the better you'll get at executing it. What's most important is that you make it your own. We all have different mannerisms, different tones of voice and we certainly don't all speak in the same way. Over time, you'll find areas to tweak, things to say that'll bring out your personality and ultimately, it'll get a lot easier and quicker to sign up clients. Whilst it may have taken some of you 15 minutes to read is section, it could have taken others 3 hours to study it. A meeting will last all of us different amounts of time but generally speaking, when you're first starting, you'll average at around 30 minutes. That being said, when you establish yourself as a market leader, you'll have a reputation, you won't need to convince businesses it's a sensible option because they will have already convinced themselves. You'll find yourself signing clients in a matter of minutes… in fact some will be begging you for your service.

For further learning on Stage 2, visit:
www.15minuteagency.com/learnmore/2

# Stage 3:

---

## How To Get Ridiculous Results For Your Clients Without Any Previous Marketing Experience.

# The 1 Thing Most Marketers Have Wrong

Before you can understand how to get results, you need to establish what you're trying to achieve. You need to understand your goals. We want to make our clients more revenue per month and we want to get them more customers. But, what's the easiest way to do that? Problem solving.

We've already gone through all of our clients problems in the meeting, so the easiest way to get them new customers is by solving their existing problems. We need to put together a list detailing each of our client's problems. Once we have formulated a list, we then need to devise individual solutions to address each of the issues they have identified. But don't overcomplicate this, it's important to solve one problem at a time. You can discuss with your client an order or priority when the kick-off meeting takes place.

Giving you an example, my first ever restaurant client once told me that Tuesdays lunchtimes were their quietest of the week. That was one of their main problems. Tuesdays were so quiet that they were doing one-tenth of the business they were doing on the rest of the week. They needed a solution as soon as possible. The client would achieve a measurable ROI from solving that one problem alone. It was the biggest gap for me to fill.

So, I was thinking, what can we do on a Tuesday lunch? How can I make them busy? I came up with a very simple tried and tested 2-4-Tuesdays offer, so it was two beef or veggie burgers for something like £15. This was the first step I was going to take to get more clients in on Tuesdays. Implementing it was another story. I knew I was going to use Facebook ads, but I didn't exactly know how to execute my targeting. Sure, I could target everybody within 2km of the restaurant, on the hopes that they'd see the ad and decide to stop for lunch. But how would I grab the attention of an audience if I was targeting everybody? So, I decided to come up with a different strategy. The restaurant was based in the centre of my local city, with tons of offices and shops around, and it came to me to target everyone who was working, to get themselves out of work for lunch. I wrote an ad that spoke directly to workers, telling them to 'sack the sandwich' and upgrade to a burger instead, introducing 2-4-Tuesdays. I remember launching two versions of the advert, one targeting my original 'everyone within 2km' with a generic message and the other, with my new 'sack the sandwich' campaign. Within two days I shut down the generic advert because the results weren't even comparable. I found myself a winner.

Writing this has reminded me of an analogy I read once, and I can't for the life of me think where it was from. It was the idea that social media is a new microphone. It said that when the first microphone was invented in 1876, lots of people started singing, although having a microphone didn't suddenly grant everyone the ability to sing. A bad singer just became an even louder bad singer when they had use of a microphone. The same principle stands for Facebook ads. You can use them to get your message in front of anyone and everyone, but just because you can, doesn't mean you'll make any money. It's the message behind the ad that counts. The right targeting and the right voice. The right voice, combined with the tools to amplify it, is the ultimate recipe for success. It's the reason my 'sack the sandwich' campaign was so successful.

With this in mind, take your time to ensure your advert campaigns captivate and relate to an audience, before you start shouting the cheapest offers from the rooftops and hoping for an uptake. Understand your client's business, their problems and any gaps that exist in the market that could offer a viable solution to their problems.

## Launching Your First Campaign

In this chapter I will run through how to create your first ever Facebook (or Instagram) ad campaign and how to navigate through the Facebook ads platform. I'll be using a series of screenshots in order to make the process a little easier. First things first, you'll need to be made admin to your clients Facebook page.

In order to do this, you'll need to ask your client to visit their business page and then using **Figure 6** as a reference:

1. Click the settings button
2. Visit page roles
3. Type your name under 'Assign a new page role'
4. Select admin from drop down
5. Click Add

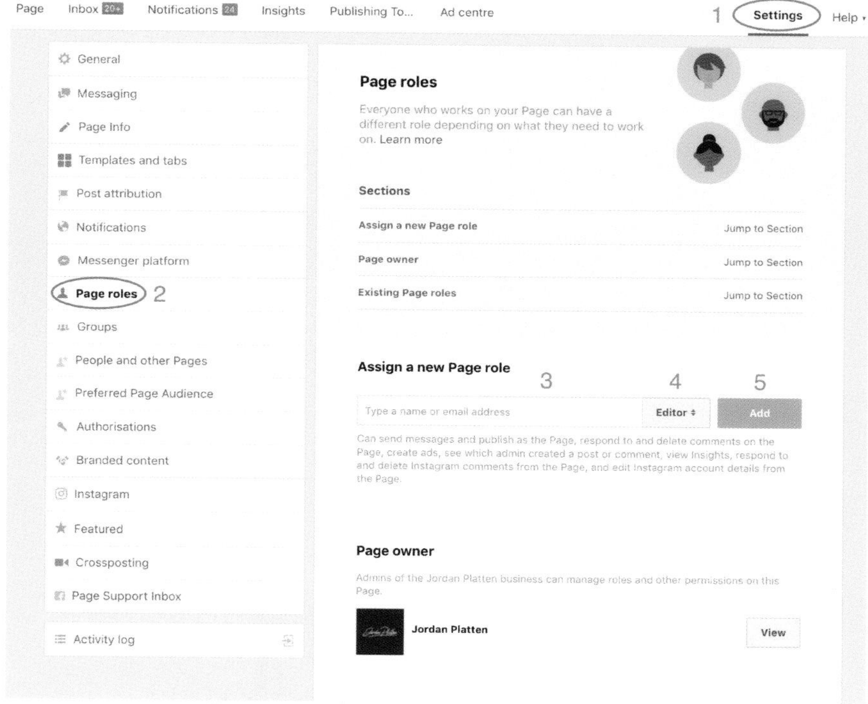


Fig. 6: Facebook business page settings

Once this is done, you'll have full access to their page. Now you need to set up Facebook business manager. Business manager is the hub where you'll manage all of your clients. We'll dive into this in a moment but first, visit business.facebook.com and set up an account. You'll be promoted to login to your Facebook profile, you may even be asked for a website URL, if you are, simply input your personal profile URL. Once you're logged in to business manager, it'll look something like **Figure 7**.

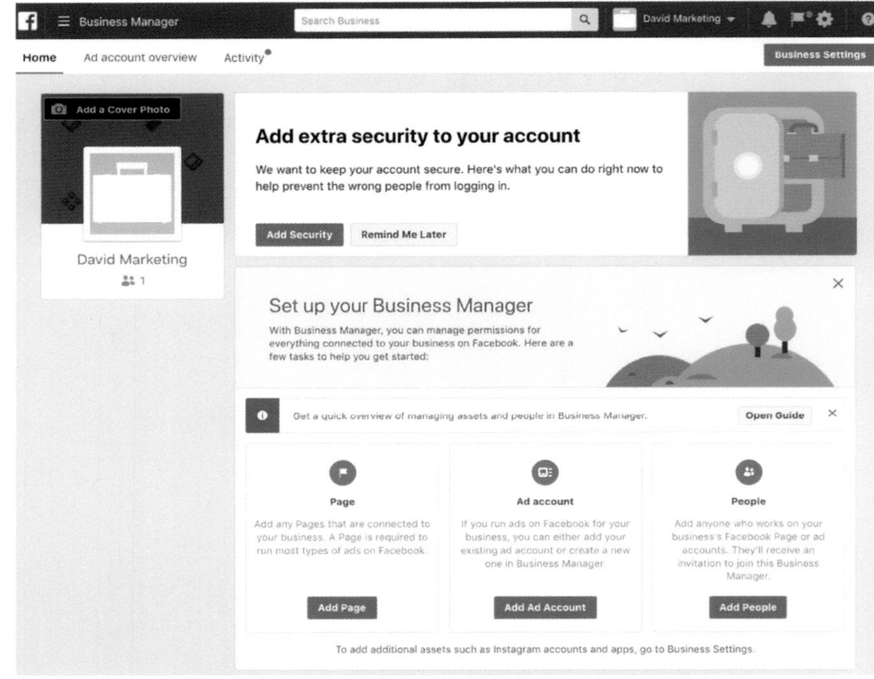


Fig. 7: Facebook business manager logged in

## To add a client's Facebook Page:

1. Click the options button (top left corner) and Click 'Business Manager Settings'
2. Under People and Assets, select 'Pages'
3. Click 'Add New Page'
4. Click 'Request Access to a Page'
5. Enter page name and make sure your role is set to 'Admin' for full access

Now the client's page is on your business manager, we need to create an ad account. This is where you'll be able to manage advertisements. You'll have a separate ad account for each client to keep everything tidy and easy to manage.

**To add an ad account to Business Manager:**

1. Open Business Manager Settings.
2. Under People and Assets, click on "Ad Accounts"
3. Select "Add New Ad Accounts"
4. Select "Create a New Ad Account" (Name it the same as your client's business name, for quick reference)

At this stage, you're pretty much good to start creating ads, but there's one final thing we need to do - set up your client's payment details on the ad account so the ad spend gets charged directly to them from Facebook **(Figure 8)**.

## To set up client payment details on Ad Account:

1. Open Settings (Not Business Manager Settings, the option just above), your page will then look like the below.
2. Select the clients ad account from the drop-down list
3. Click 'Add People' and type your clients personal name (you will need to be friends with them on Facebook), you will need to assign them the role of admin
4. Click 'Payment Settings'. This will take you to another page
5. Take the URL from the payment settings page and send it to your client
6. Client will need to click the big 'Add payment method' button and input their card details

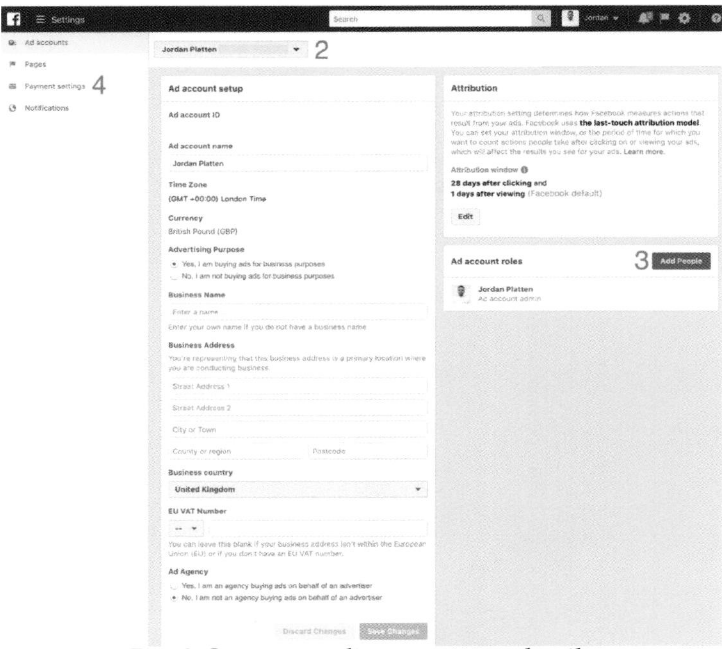


Fig. 8: Setting up client payment details

For security, you will not be able to see any details regarding your client's payment details, so you can assure them of that if necessary.

This completes the set up process for your first ever client. Let's move onto creating your first ever ad campaign. Firstly, you should understand the structure of the Facebook advertising platform. I've included a diagram below to explain. Imagine Business Manager as the umbrella over everything, it's the hub for managing all of your clients. Inside Business Manager we have Ads Manager, which hosts a number of ad accounts. It is good practice to have an ad account for each of your clients. Never manage more than one client from one ad account, otherwise it'll get extremely messy. Inside the ad accounts we have our ads, which are broken down into 3 sections. Campaigns, which are our objectives (we already touched on this in the meeting strategy). Ad sets, which is the targeting and finally, Ads or Ad copy, which is the creative side of the advert. This is what your client's potential customers will see on their newsfeeds.

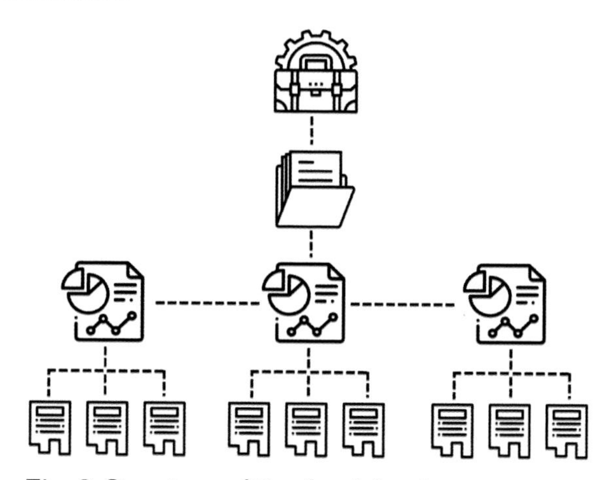

Fig. 9: Structure of Facebook business manager

To create your first ad campaign, visit options and click Ads Manager. Your page will look like **Figure 10**. Don't be daunted by this page, it looks an awful lot more complicated than it actually is. Here you can see in the centre of the page, we have Campaigns, Ad Sets and Ads. Of course, these are all empty currently but if you need to access any of them in the future, it's easy to do so.

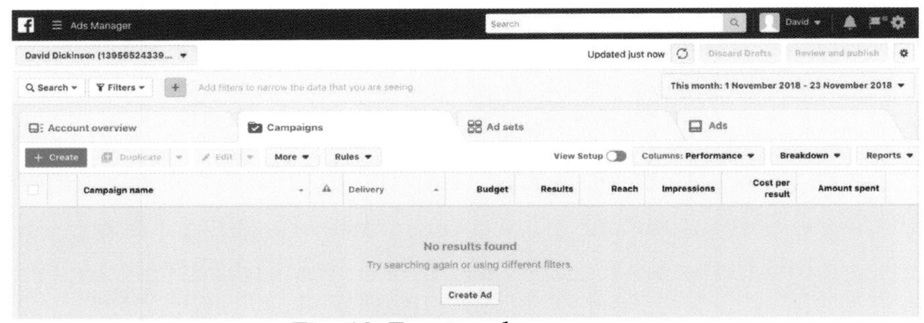

Fig. 10: Empty ads manager

In order to create an ad, click either the central grey or left hand side green 'Create Ad' buttons, it doesn't matter which. You'll be taken to the campaign creation page, which will be familiar to you **(Figure 4)**. You will then select your ad objective. You'll also be prompted to name your campaign at the bottom of the page. Make it something memorable yet functional, for example "Traffic - Reservations". Click continue.

We're now taken through to the Ad Set stage **(Figure 11)**, which requires you to define your audience. Generally speaking, for your first ad, you're not going to need to play with any settings until you get to the Audience tab. Working our way down from top to bottom, we have custom audiences. Custom audiences are typically created after working with a client for a certain period of time and can be very useful for retargeting. For example, custom audiences can be created to retarget all website visitors within a set time period, or audiences can be created to retarget people who visit the 'add to cart' page but abandon the process before completing the purchase. For now, you don't need to worry about these but if it's something that you want to explore further, it is something that I've covered extensively in a separate training course.

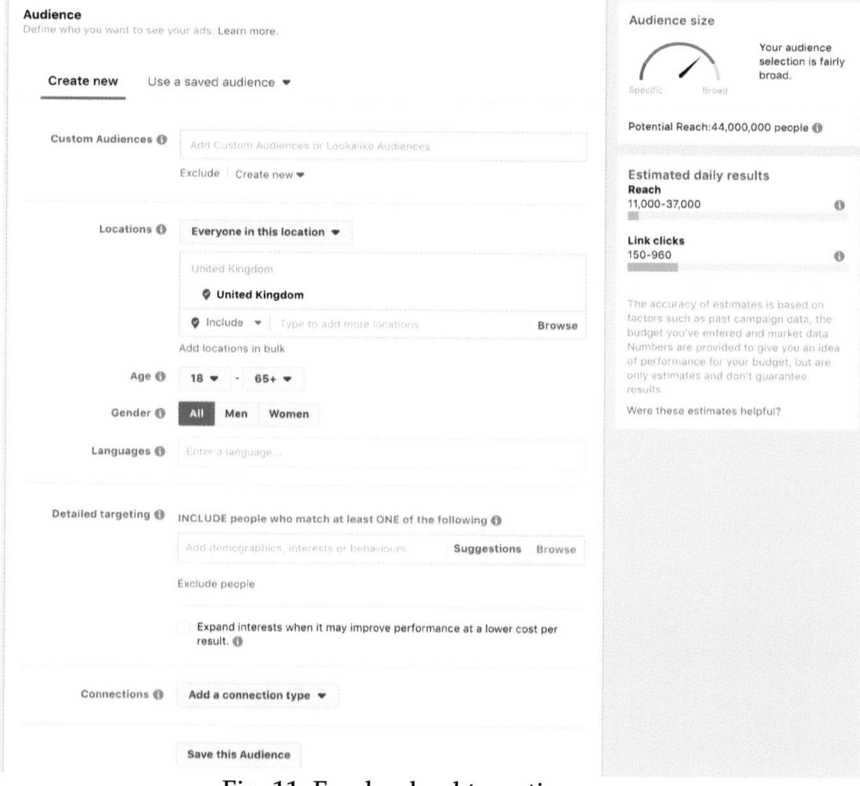


Fig. 11: Facebook ad targeting page

Moving on, we have locations, which is pretty self explanatory, we are simply selecting the geographical area we wish to target. We can firstly select whether we want to target everybody inside a location, everybody who lives inside, is travelling inside or is just passing by. This can be particularly useful for Dentists for example, where you would have no interest in targeting an audience who don't live in the local area.

We then have the options to select Age, Gender, Languages and finally, detailed targeting (which we've already covered). I thoroughly recommend that you play around with detailed targeting when you first get started by clicking on the 'Browse' button. In this section you will discover a whole range of targeting options that you have probably never even considered. We also have the ability to exclude people from our audience, which is useful when trying to narrow down to a very specific audience.

Below this, using the Connections tab, we can exclude or include people who are linked to certain pages. If for instance we were launching a campaign in the hope of attracting more page likes, we would want to exclude everybody who already likes our client's page.

Moving on further down the page, we have Placements **(Figure 12)**. This is where you select exactly where you would like your clients adverts to be displayed. I would always advise against using automatic placements because Facebook will often just show your ads in the cheapest possible places, without much consideration to whether they're the most effective or relevant. Click edit placements to bring up the list seen in the screenshot below. In this option you will find a selection of all the possibilities, including the ability to create an Instagram ad too, with the simple tick of a box. Generally speaking, 90% of ads perform best on the Facebook feed only, but this of course completely depends on the context and purpose of the ad, but certainly for traffic and engagement, it's king. This is simply because feed ads are the ones that closely reflect organic posts that you see on your newsfeed every day.

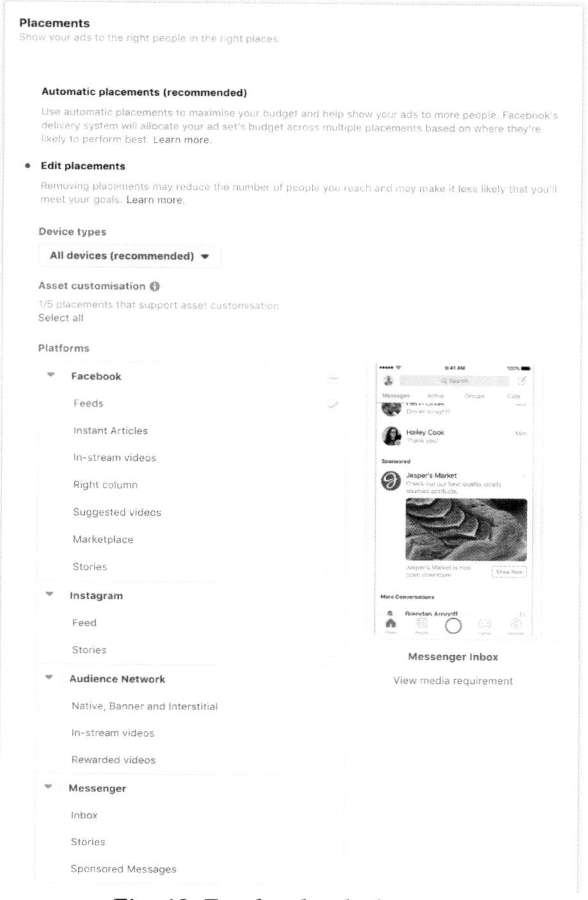


Fig. 12: Facebook ad placements

Finishing up on Ad Sets, we have our budget and schedule **(Figure 13)**. Going from the top down again, is the ad budget, this can be configured for either daily or lifetime. 95% of the time, your ads will be on a daily budget as you'll have more control over what your client is spending. I would always recommend starting ads on a £5 per day advert budget and scaling up once they start performing well.

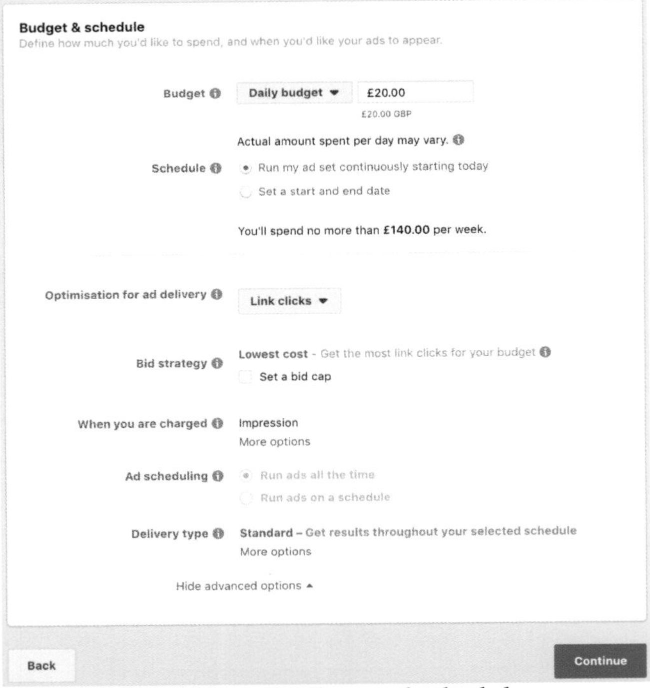


Fig. 13: Ad budget and schedule

Next is the schedule. This can be particularly useful if you would like to schedule a number of ads in advance and preselect start and end dates so the changeover is autonomous.

Then finally in Fig.13 we have optimisation. You will very rarely have to change this because Facebook is particularly good at optimising everything for you. That being said, there are occasions where you will want to change link clicks to conversions, particularly with e-commerce clients where your goal is to get web purchases. Now we've covered pretty much everything inside of ad sets, simply click continue and we'll be taken to the final stage of ad creation - the ad copy.

After clicking continue, you'll be brought to the Ad creation page **(Figure 14)**. This is where you'll bring an ad to life and create what the world will see on their newsfeeds.

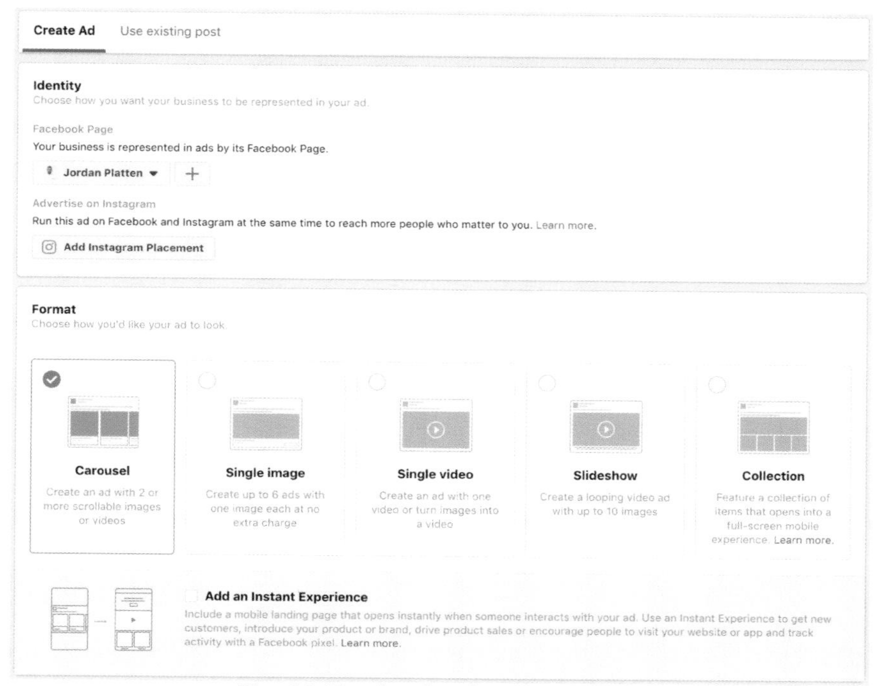


Fig. 14: Facebook ad creation page

The first option we'll be given is whether we want to create a new ad or use an existing post. It's important to note that ads created through ad manager won't be seen on your client's page, they'll only be visible on the placements of your selected audience. Although if you click 'use existing post' you'll be able to create ads from existing page posts, which will mean page visitors will be able to see the ads too, not just the target audience. This is ideal for engagement ads.

Moving on to the identify tab, it's important to make sure that your client's page and/or Instagram pages are selected, we don't want to accidentally run ads for one client on a different client's page.

Then we have format. This is where we select the visuals for the ad that we'd like to run. I'd recommend having a play with these and getting a feel for what works. All formats have their own purpose. For example a carousel ad, which is essentially a series of photos, would be an excellent choice for e-commerce businesses who have a series of products to showcase, or it would be great for a restaurant where the various dishes could be displayed.

Further down the page you will find the images and the creative, both of which are used to design our desired advert **(Figure 15)**. As you can see on the right hand side of the screenshot, we are given a live preview of our advert depending on what data we input. This is really useful because you can see it exactly as the target audience will see it. Just above that we can also select whether we'd like to preview a desktop or mobile version.

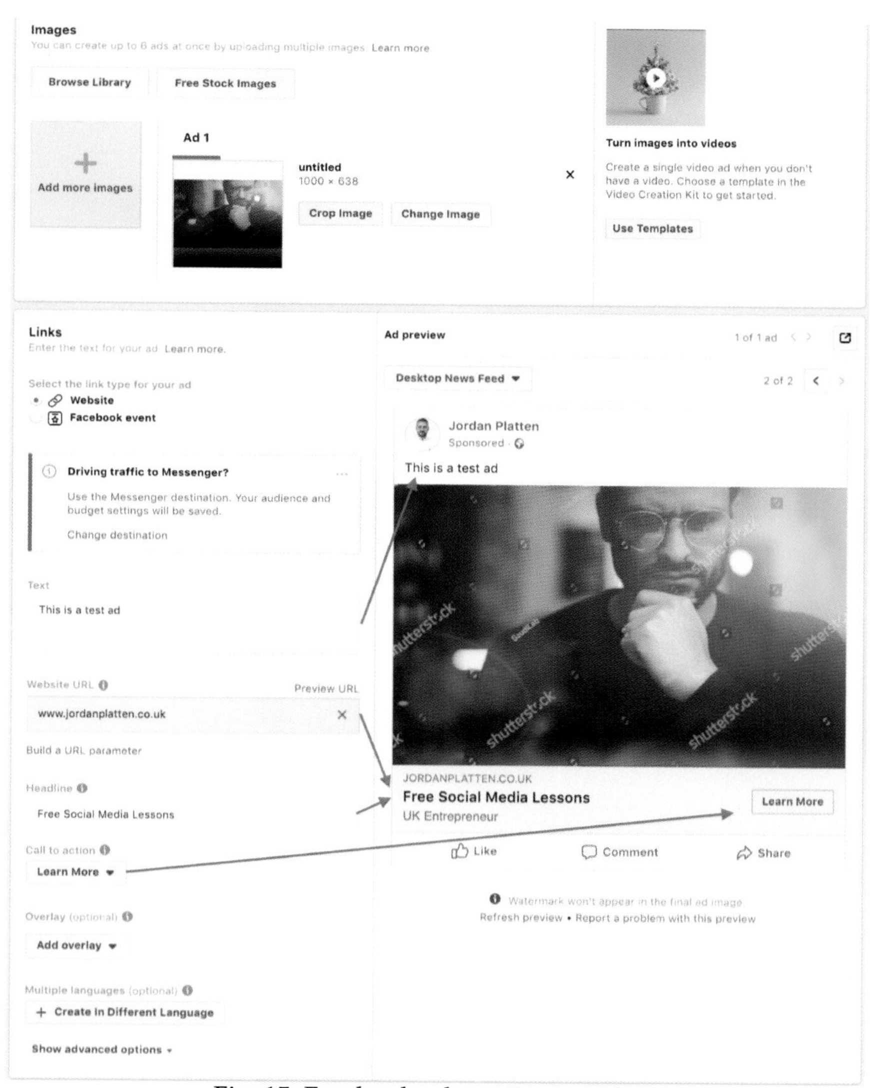

Fig. 15: Facebook ad creation preview

This page is pretty self explanatory and again I encourage you to have a play, but for the purpose of demonstration I've linked individual fields to their corresponding creative change.

It's important to point out that the Website URL is the URL we're trying to drive traffic to with this advert. Another useful tool to mention is the Call to Action, which can be edited using the drop down on the left. Every ad should have one of these. A call to action is the specific action that you would like the audience to take. Typical calls to action include 'Buy Now', 'Subscribe', 'Limited Availability, Book Today'. This is a great tool for prompting your audience to click the ad. When you combine a call to action with a sense of urgency, exclusivity or limited availability, it will further compel the person seeing the ad to click the link and take the action that you want them to take. Writing an effective ad is part art, part science and as you become more skilled in creating ads you will improve your skills in writing copy and creating ads that convert.

I've also taken a screenshot of the ad copy page for an engagement advert, so you can compare the differences **(Figure 16)**. You'll notice that in comparison to traffic, it's much simpler. This is because engagement ads are simply text and either images or videos. After you're happy with your advert's design, simply scroll to the bottom of the page and hit confirm.

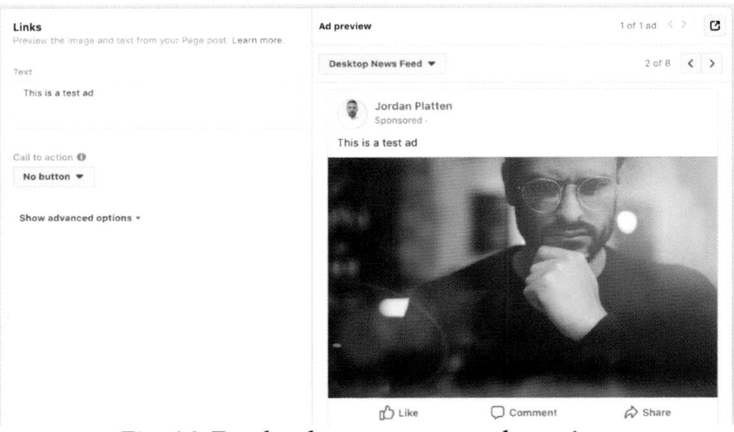


Fig. 16: Facebook engagement ad preview

Once your first ad has been created, you'll be taken back to the ad account, where you'll find your newly created ad **(Figure 17)**. Typically, under the delivery tab, the advert will be 'in review' for up to 24hrs until it's approved by Facebook's algorithm. It'll then change to active and your first advert will be live. If you wish to edit any component of your at any time, you can do by clicking either campaign, ad sets or ads, hovering over the ad name and clicking edit.

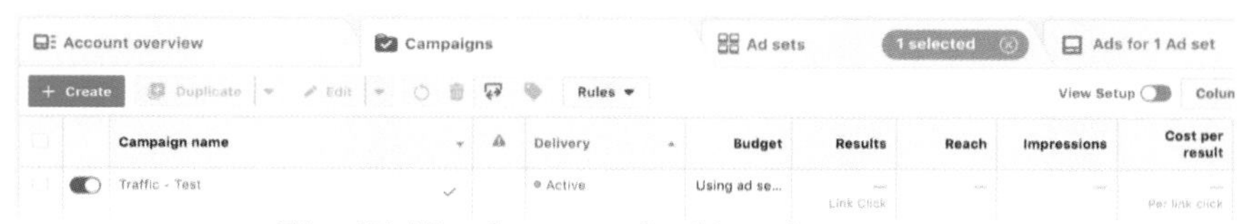


Fig. 17: Newly created ad in ads manager

Creating powerful ads is a skill that comes with both knowledge and time, you now know how to set up your first client and create your first ever advert campaign for them. As I've mentioned throughout this chapter, I recommend you to have a play with ads manager yourself, familiarising yourself with its workings. Knowing how to create ads is one thing but understanding how to sign clients and promote their message to the world is another. This training has taught you just that. However, with this in mind, how good is your voice? In the next chapter, I'm going to give you some singing lessons.

# The Secret Formula For Creating Ads That'll Sell Ice To Eskimos

Knowing what to write alongside your ads can be difficult, especially when you haven't created any before. Luckily for you, you get to skip out all of the countless hours I wasted testing different variables in order to find what works. There is much debate in the Facebook ad world regarding how you should structure an ad, some say long copy is best, others say short. Some say provide value, others say keep the audience asking questions. The truth is, it's completely client specific. What works for one client just won't work for another. That being said, since launching my agency, myself and my team ensure that we include 5 key elements in 90% of our revenue generating ads. What do I mean by revenue generating ads? I'm talking traffic, conversion, lead generation, anything where the sole purpose of the ad is for the audience to convert into a sale.

### 1. Attention Grabber

How many times have you flicked through your feed so quickly, merely skimming through content without stopping? Pretty much all of us. Statistics prove that if a Facebook post doesn't captivate your attention within the first few words, you're going to skip past. That's why it's vitally important we directly connect with our audience right away.

### 2. The What

Get straight to the point. Nobody likes having their time wasted and frankly, no-one is going to read past the first or second line of an ad if they don't yet know what it's about. Your audience must immediately know what the ad is about.

### 3. The Why

Why do your audience need your offer? Your ad has to be relevant. Tell your audience why your product or service is a no-brainer.

### 4. Curiosity Factor / Scarcity

Throw them off guard. Include a surprising fact / statistic or make your offer limited to a set number of people. Make your audience feel like they're missing out on something or by taking you up on your offer you are giving them something exclusive or valuable.

### 5. Call To Action

People like being told what to do, it's human nature. Tell your audience exactly what they need to do to redeem your offer or buy your product / service and tell them to do it now through your Call to Action

In addition to the above, from personal experience I have found that shorter ad copy will work best whilst trying to sell. Try to avoid your audience having to click the 'see more' button on your ad. We want them to see all of the relevant information in one place. Engagement adverts on the other hand, are much simpler. In fact, the shorter the ad copy the better. Let your media do the talking. If for example you're working with a restaurant, simply describe the dish, making it sound as sexy as possible of course.

Above all, make sure what you're advertising is desirable for your audience. With the correct offer, audience and the inclusion of the above 5 elements, you can be sure of a successful campaign.

For further learning on Stage 3, visit:
www.15minuteagency.com/learnmore/3

# The Key To How I Scaled To 6 Figures In Less Than 3 Months

When I launched my agency in 2017, I scaled to a 6 figure business (around £9,500 a month) in less than 3 months. This wasn't down to fluke, nor was it to luck, it was simply down to my burning desire to succeed, no matter what the cost. Before launching my agency, I was miserable, desperately trying to keep my head above water, trying to find a way to escape my 9-5. The moment I caught wind of a business model that would work for me, I didn't look back. I remember waking up at 5am, educating myself until 6am, going to the gym, coming home and learning some more before rushing off to work, prospecting on my lunch break, rushing back home and spending all evening cold calling local businesses. I repeated this process every day for two weeks and within that period I managed to sign my first two clients worth £2,000 a month. I did what others say they 'don't have time' to do. Yes. I was burnt out, yes, I was fed up, but I didn't stop until I had made enough money to quit my job and the day I quit was the best day of my life. I was euphoric. I've never looked back.

As a social media marketer, having a growth strategy is essential. You need to set specific daily and weekly targets that you adhere to religiously. This is absolutely essential if you wish to grow quickly. Targets also motivate you and keep you on track; you will feel guilty if you don't stick to them. The targets I'm about to discuss are the exact targets I followed when I first launched my agency, on the basis of scaling at the same rate I did (although you can do it much, much quicker. I've had students do it in far less).

Firstly, a six figure agency is essentially nine clients paying £1,000 pounds per month each. Now, that's the minimum service charge that we want to go for. Really, we want to be aiming for £1,500, £2,000+ or even more than that depending on the clients. Nine clients is the absolute maximum that we need to hit six figures. Now, on this basis, that's around £108,000 per year. Nine clients divided by three months, that's only three clients we need to obtain per month.

If you're using cold calls as your main strategy for securing meetings, you would need to make on average 20 cold calls per day. This is Monday to Friday. Now don't get scared by these figures, 20 cold calls is not a lot at all. That'll probably just take you an hour or two max. Some of these phone calls will only be about 20 seconds long, you'll speak to the gatekeeper, they'll tell you the business owner isn't in, you end the call, and call them back another day. From experience, out of those 20 cold calls, you'll speak to an average of five owners. Why won't you speak to every single owner? It goes without saying that sometimes they won't be in, sometimes they will be busy, or sometimes they simply won't have the time to speak to you. Out of those 5 business owners, again, from experience by rule of averages, you're looking at around one meeting set. So, if we extrapolate that over the course of a week, that's 100 cold calls a week, 25 owners on the phone, five meetings set, and from those five meetings, if you follow the meeting strategy correctly, you should be able to sign multiple clients. I signed my first 2/2 meetings until I had a rejection on my third. Naturally, some of you will find it easier to secure clients than others, whilst some of you will need a little bit of practice.

It's important you don't get disheartened if you don't convert at the same figures mentioned above. 20 calls in a rural area simply isn't going to be the same as 20 calls in a big city, as companies will be getting called more frequently. In addition to this, rejection is normal, if you're new to business it's something you'll have to get used to. Not every business you meet will see eye to eye with you. That's just part of life.

At the end of the day, the rate you grow is in your own hands, if you wish to take breaks, you can. In fact, I took many days off when I first started. I fell in love with the new found freedom. It all boils down to your own personal goals, your own personal ambitions and what you want from your business. In the end, if you can condition yourself to stay focused, handle rejections, be resilient and stick to targets, you'll be unstoppable.

# Conclusion

We're there, at the end of the book, but the learning certainly doesn't end here. I admit, there's a lot of information to take in at once, so I'd advise going over each chapter again until its ingrained in your mind. Read it often and really study the material in this book. Repetition is the key to success. Go back to it even when you have started signing clients and keep it fresh in your mind. Read the chapters as you go along.

When I first started, I was crying out for a tool like this, for someone to show me the ropes and lay everything out on the table. Instead, I read multiple books, watched tons of YouTube videos and invested thousands in mentorship with 7 figure marketing agency owners in the hopes of piecing everything together. Whilst I managed to find success quickly, it wasn't an easy route for me. That is precisely why I wrote the 15 Minute Agency, so others wouldn't have to muddle through like I did.

Learning doesn't have to stop at the 15 Minute Agency though, in fact, we're at the tip of the iceberg. Those of you who have seen my content will know in mid 2018 I launched a fully fledged online marketing school. It has since become one of the fastest growing online training schools in the world, with hundreds of enrolled students, from all walks of life.

It is my life-long mission to help others who are hungry for success, to escape the rat race of employment and start their own business. Through the Social Media Marketing School, I've hosted over 60 fully comprehensive video lessons, walking through the entire process of building a rapidly scalable social media agency from the ground up, including all of my in-depth marketing strategies used for clients, with new content being added monthly. In addition to this, all members get full access to personal mentorship from me, through both the exclusive student community and 1-on-1 through my personal channels.

In fact, I'd like to invite you over to the school, to become part of our incredible community of rapidly growing entrepreneurs. Visit www.socialmediamarketing.school to learn more.

I hope you've enjoyed the contents of this book. I've now given you the tools to change, it's time to take action, grab your life by the balls, and live how you've always dreamed of living. Start your journey today and make this the beginning of something great. I cannot wait to hear of your success.

Jordan Platten

www.jordanplatten.co.uk